HISTORY MYSTERIES

Vol. 1

by Richard Kimbrough

Royal Fireworks Press

Unionville, New York

Royal Fireworks Press
First Avenue, PO Box 399
Unionville, NY 10988-0399
(845) 726-4444
FAX: (845) 726-3824
e-mail: rfpress@frontiernet.net

ISBN: 0-88092-191-9 Paperback

Printed in the United States of America by the Royal Fireworks
Press of Unionville, New York.

WHAT ARE
HISTORY MYSTERIES?

Once a teacher discovered a student reading a mystery novel while she was supposed to be studying her history lesson. "Why do you do this?" asked the teacher, disappointed at the student's errant behavior.

"Because I like mysteries," explained the student. "Mysteries have suspense. Mysteries have excitement. Mysteries have...well, mystery. History is so dry and dull, just dates and facts and names and all that stuff. No suspense, no excitement, no mystery."

"Well, perhaps it seems that way to you," allowed the teacher, "but, really, history has mystery, too, you know."

"History has mystery?" The student was doubtful.

"Yes. I'll show you. I'll put together some history mysteries that you can solve, little mysteries from American history."

"How do I solve them?" asked the student.

"The same way any detective solves mysteries. You start with some information, and you search for more. You make use of the library, hunt in books that seem promising sources, ask questions of your teachers, your friends, your parents, your grandparents, anyone who might have information that will help you solve the mystery. You persist in the way a good detective does. You don't give up until you have the solution."

"Well, I don't know..." said the student, still doubtful.

"I'll have some history mysteries ready for you to solve by next week," promised the teacher.

So here are the history mysteries that the teacher prepared. Can you solve them?

THE OLDEST FORT

For one hundred years, commanders of this settlement located in the New World wrote letter after letter to Mexico City and Madrid asking for money to construct a stone fort. There was a wooden fort already built protecting the settlement. Indeed, over the years there were nine wooden forts, all of which fell victim to fire, hurricanes, or termites.

But the authorities in Mexico City and Madrid saw no need for a stone fort. Nothing of importance happened at this remote outpost. A wooden fort offered plenty of protection.

Then in 1688 a ship manned by a crew from another country, a country that was the great enemy of Spain, captured the wooden fort and the settlement around it. Before long, these captors left, but they made it plain that they would be back. Moreover, people from this other country built a fort of their own to the north.

Now, alarmed, the Spanish government ordered the viceroy of Mexico to pay for a stone fort, and by 1695 a stone fort called the Castillo de San Marcos was completed.

The Castillo de San Marcos stands to this day, guarding the only walled city in the United States.

What city does the fort guard?

From what country were the people who raided the settlement in 1688?

What city did these people establish to the north in 1670?

WASHINGTON'S BIRTHDAY

Let us suppose for a moment that George Washington were reincarnated and came back to visit a class of fifth graders. During the course of the conversation, one of the students might say, "President Washington, we celebrate your birthday, you know, February 22."

And Washington might answer, "You do? On February 22? That's not the date on which I was born."

Well, when was Washington born?

AN ENGLISH PREACHER

In 1739 an Englishman came to America who spoke to huge gatherings of people throughout the colonies. Most of the leaders among his profession in America refused to let him speak in their buildings; thus, he stood in the middle of fields and delivered his message. He was a tremendously persuasive speaker with a clear, booming voice.

One prominent American who heard this Englishman wrote, "I happened…to attend one of his [speeches], in the course of which I perceived he intended to [ask his listeners for money]. I resolved that he would get nothing from me. I had in my pocket a handful of copper money, three or four dollars, and five pistoles in gold. As he proceeded I began to soften and concluded to give him the copper. Another stroke of his oratory made me ashamed of that, and determined me to give the silver; and he finished so admirably, that I emptied my pocket wholly into the collector's dish, gold and all."

Who was this Englishman who could persuade his audience to give their money so generously?

Who was the American who gave the money?

What was the time of this Englishman's visit to America called?

THE FIRST TO DIE

Following are two quotations about the same man and the same incident in American history. We've left out a name here and there and some other information, but you can still solve the mystery.

"[This man] was the first to give his life in [this war] as he tried to rally the Americans that night."

"When [this man] waved his cordwood club and urged the crowd forward, someone gave the order to fire and the British muskets cut down [this man] and four other Bostonians."

Who was this man who was the first to give his life?

What was the incident?

When did the incident occur?

Of which war are we speaking and when did it actually start?

THE EMBLEM

A very famous American once wrote about the following creature as an emblem to be placed on a flag: "I ran over in my mind every property by which she was distinguished.

"I recollected that her eye excelled in brightness that of any other animal, and that she has no eye-lids—she may therefore be esteemed an emblem of vigilance.—She never begins an attack, nor, when once engaged, ever surrenders: She is therefore an emblem of magnanimity and true courage.—As if anxious to prevent all pretensions of quarreling with her, the weapons with which nature has furnished her, she conceals in the roof of her mouth, so that, to those who are unacquainted with her, she appears to be a most defenseless animal; and even when those weapons are shown and extended for her defense, they appear weak and contemptible; but their wounds however small, are decisive and fatal:—Conscious of this, she never wounds till she has generously given notice, even to her enemy, and cautioned him against the danger..."

What creature is being discussed as an emblem?

What famous American wrote about this creature as an emblem?

What ever happened to his idea of using this creature as an emblem?

AMERICA'S POLISH REVOLUTIONARY

A brilliant young Polish military engineer named Thaddeus Kosciusko contributed significantly to the success of the American Revolution. Among his many achievements, he laid out the American army's positions before the battle of Saratoga and in doing so assured the colonists' success in the battle that proved the turning point of the war. He also planned and supervised the building of the defenses at West Point, making that fort on the Hudson River nearly unassailable, and, one more thing, he plotted the successful escape of Nathanael Greene's Southern Army from the clutches of the British General Cornwallis and his forces.

At the war's end, General George Washington honored the young Pole by inviting him to be present when he bade farewell to his top officers, and the Congress recognized Kosciusko's "long, faithful, and meritorious service."

Now to the mystery: why did Kosciusko leave his homeland and come to America in the first place?

A FOUNDING FATHER

One of the most prominent of the Founding Fathers of this country came to New York in 1773. He became a captain in the artillery in 1776 and bravely led his men against the British commander Lord Cornwallis at the second battle of Trenton. In 1777 he became the aide-de-camp to General Washington and was sent on several important military missions.

After the Revolutionary War this man led the call for a Constitutional Convention, and when it was held he was a delegate. He authored many of the Federalist Papers urging citizens to affirm the Constitution. When the new government was launched in 1789, President Washington appointed him to an important cabinet position. His financial program and his Report on Manufactures were instrumental in setting the course for the new nation and still influence many of our economic ideas. He was America's first great nationalist, and his efforts were always toward making America strong and prosperous.

Well, you won't have much difficulty learning the identity of this Founding Father. But there's something else: had it not been for a most stormy event, this great patriot might never have come to North America.

Who was this man, and what was the event that propelled him to North America?

POPULATING A CONTINENT

The unexpected victory of the American colonists over the British in the Revolutionary War had a great effect, of course, on two continents, Europe and North America, but it also had a considerable effect on a third continent. In fact, the American victory served to populate this third continent.

What was the third continent?

Why did the colonists' victory help to populate it?

SLAVE AND ANTI-SLAVE

For many years American history textbooks have told the remarkable story of an American inventor who created two things: one of which caused slavery to be fastened upon the South, and thus was in large measure responsible for the coming of the Civil War; the second of which gave the North the means to win the Civil War. (Today there is some doubt as to how successful his company was with the second creation, but in any event, he did promote the idea of this second development.)

Who was this inventor?

What were his two creations?

THE GREAT LEADER

At a time when this great leader was seeking to organize a confederation of many nations, a group from one of the nations appeared and demanded proof that the leader's brother could really predict the future accurately. The brother had long claimed that he could.

The leader secretly instructed his brother to tell the group that in 50 days the sky would turn black at high noon, the night creatures would stir, and the stars would shine.

When the prediction came true, the people of all the nations believed in the prophet and in his brother, the leader.

But the leader still had troubles. A girl named Rebecca Galloway taught him to read and write English, and they fell in love. She agreed to marry him only if he became like her people. He said that he could not do that, that if he did he would lose the respect of his people. So sadly he and the girl he loved parted.

The leader met with another nation's general, a nation that was seeking to take the land of the leader's people, and when their negotiations regarding ownership of the land failed, the leader told the general, "I suppose that you and I will have to fight it out."

When the leader was away on another mission, urged on by his brother the prophet, his people attacked the general's forces. The general's troops won.

When the leader returned, he was so angered by his brother's actions that he shook him by the hair until his nose bleed and then banished him from camp.

Who was this great leader?

What nations did he lead?

How was the leader able to predict accurately that the sky would turn black at high noon?

What ever happened to the leader?

A TREASURED PRODUCT

Frederic Tudor, Samuel Austin, Jr., and William C. Rogers are names little known in American history. Yet together they owned a company which made a fortune selling a certain New England product in the far corners of the world. This product was especially popular in India during the time that the British governed that subcontinent. While it was used medically, perhaps more importantly it was treasured because it permitted a greater variety of food and provided a bit of luxury in a hostile climate. Straw was used to transport the product.

So highly prized as this product supplied by Tudor, Austin, and Rogers that Lord William Bentinck, the British Governor-General of India, presented Rogers a large silver loving cup as a thank you for introducing it to India.

. What was this product?

CURED BY LOVE

Sophia was one of three remarkable sisters. All were highly intelligent and wonderfully talented. Sadly, however, Sophia's talent could not be fully realized. A landscape artist of considerable ability, she felt such sensitivity to natural beauty that usually she was so overwhelmed by it that she could not paint. Indeed, the wonders of nature made her physically ill, and until she was in her late 20's, she was ill most of the time, suffering from fever, lameness, and other problems.

Her sister Elizabeth invited a novelist to visit, but Sophia was upstairs ill when the guest arrived and did not get to meet him. However, she read his books and drew a picture of one of his characters which she later showed him. He liked it, and, more importantly, he liked her. In fact, he loved her. And she, in turn, loved him.

But alas, the author's mother and sisters opposed the romance because they feared his marriage would keep him from writing. Sophia was concerned, too, that she should not ask her beloved to take time away from his writing to care for her? And he worried that he did not make enough money to support her.

But after a four-year engagement, they set a wedding date. However, she became quite ill with a high fever before the wedding, and it had to be postponed four weeks. But at last they were married. His mother and sisters did not attend the wedding.

Marriage agreed with Sophia. Her health improved until it was excellent. She and her novelist husband had three children and a most happy life until when he was 56 years old his health failed mysteriously.

What was Sophia's maiden name?

What was her married name?

Who was her husband?

Who were Sophia's famous sisters?

To whom was her sister Mary married?

THE PECULIAR PEOPLE

During the 1800's and into the early 1900's, most Americans who came in contact with them thought that these people who formed a small religious sect were a little strange. To cite some examples of their peculiarities: they did not believe in marriage thus the sexes were carefully segregated; they always lined up in a certain order before they entered a room; they were required to step first on the right foot when going upstairs; they always piled chicken bones in an exact way on their plates.

Yet in many ways they were ahead of their time. They banned slavery in their villages in 1817; they owned automobiles before most other people in their areas; they were among the first Americans to use electricity widely. They were great inventors. Among their inventions were clothespins, wigs, circular saws, and washing machines.

Today these people are gone, and most Americans who remember them do so only because of the style of furniture that they created and which still exists today.

Who were these strange people?

FRIENDS OR ENEMIES

As he lay dying, a former President of the United States sent farewell messages to his three dearest friends. One of these messages went to a Missouri Senator. For several reasons, it was not surprising that the dying man should count the Missouri Senator among his friends. Earlier in their careers, the man now Senator had been the dying man's chief aide at one of the most famous battles in American history, a battle later popularized by a country-western song. The Senator had led the dying man's forces in the Senate when the latter had been President. He had defended the dying man against charges that he had violated the Constitution while President.

He had written a much-read history praising the dying man as a great man and a great President. Yet for one reason it was quite astonishing that the dying man should count the Senator among his friends at all, let alone among his dearest friends. Indeed, because of that reason, you might logically imagine that the Senator would have been among the dying man's foremost *enemies*.

Who was the ex-President?

Who was the Missouri Senator?

For what reason might the Senator have been among the dying man's foremost enemies?

By the way, can you name the very famous relative of the Missouri Senator's? On what talent was his fame based?

Finally, what battle was popularized by the country-western song?

AMERICA'S GREATEST ORATOR

At birth she was given the name Isabella. Her early life was filled with great hardship. She owned literally nothing of her own into adulthood. The mother of five children, she saw four of those children taken from her. Promised a most valuable gift on July 4, 1827, she had this gift withheld from her at the last moment.

Yet she persisted. Befriended by a family named Van Wagener, she took the name Isabella Van Wagener, and she sued in court to regain custody of her son Peter, then five years old. Amazingly, against all odds, the courts found in Isabella's favor and returned her son to her.

Even more surprisingly when she later sued a prominent New York businessman for slandering her—the man had spread the story that Isabella had tried to poison him and his wife—she won the suit and was awarded 125 dollars, then a handsome sum.

And as the years passed, despite her lack of formal knowledge of the English language—after all, she had never had the opportunity to attend school—she became a tremendously powerful speaker who aroused great passions in her audiences. Most people think that Senator Daniel Webster of Massachusetts was the nation's greatest orator, but perhaps this Isabella moved audiences even more than Webster.

In 1850 she told her life story to a friend who put it down in book form. The book became an immediate bestseller, and along with Harriet Beecher Stowe's *Uncle Tom's Cabin,* greatly influenced subsequent national events.

By what name is Isabella Van Wagener known in history? Why was it so remarkable that she won her lawsuits?

A GIFT FOR HIS PEOPLE

Once there was a member of the Cherokee tribe living in Tennessee who took part in all the activities of the men in his tribe until one day he suffered a hunting accident which left him crippled and unable to hunt and work as he had before.

Thereafter, he began to leave his family almost daily to go into the woods and arrange small bits of wood in patterns or mark on stone. At first his fellow tribesmen merely thought that he was a bit strange but when he kept doing odd things year after year for twelve years, they came to believe that he was totally crazy.

But the truth was that this peculiar man had noticed something quite amazing when he had dealt with white men, and he was spending his time thinking about what he had noticed.

Then one day, using his small daughter in his demonstration, he showed the chiefs of the tribe the fruits of his years of labor. In an instant all of them saw what a great and wonderous man they had in their midst.

Who was this Cherokee tribesman?

What was it that he had noticed about white men?

What had he created in his years of work?

THE INVENTION

The great artist had worked so long and hard on his invention, and now he was sure that he had it perfected. The only obstacle was that he lacked the money to put it into operation. At last he all but persuaded the Congress of the United States to appropriate $30,000 to put up the necessary equipment; however, Congress delayed and it appeared that the artist must wait another year before his invention could be tested. With Congress hours from adjournment for the year, and the appropriation bill not voted upon, the artist went to bed, bitterly disappointed.

The next morning a young lady named Annie Ellsworth came to see the artist. She told him that Congress had passed his bill.

He protested, saying, "You are mistaken. My Senatorial friends assured me that there was no chance for me."

"But it is you who are mistaken," she replied. "My father was at the adjournment at midnight and saw the President sign your bill."

So delighted was the artist that he promised Annie Ellsworth that she might write the first words to be associated with his invention.

Who was the artist?

What was his invention?

What words did Miss Ellsworth write?

AMERICA'S PASTIME

Baseball is called America's Pastime. It grew out of a game played in England called rounders. During the 1840's New York businessmen played rounders on their noon hour and after work, but they wished that the game could more fully challenge the ability of players to hit, throw, catch, and run, the basic physical activities of humans. In other works, rounders was too tame for these men.

Then one day someone thought of a basic change that could be made in rounders that would make it more challenging.

What was that basic change, so simple but so important, that changed rounders into baseball?

IMMORTALITY IS A FIFTEEN MINUTE POEM

One of the earliest and most successful advocates of women's rights in America was a most remarkable woman who lived in the Nineteenth Century. Left a young widow in 1822, she raised five children, all of whom enjoyed distinguished careers, wrote 24 books, raised money to complete the Bunker Hill Monument in Boston, helped found the Seaman's Aid Society to assist sailors and their families, and for 47 years edited *Godey's Lady's Book*, the most influential women's magazine in the nation. Along with Harriet Beecher Stowe, the author of *Uncle Tom's Cabin,* this woman influenced American life more than any other woman of the Nineteenth Century.

Yet for all her great work, this woman is most remembered for a short piece of writing she dashed off in 15 minutes one day. All of you probably know this writing by heart.

Who was the woman, and what did she write?

THE RECLUSE AND
THE LETTER

On July 23, 1864, Miss Emily Hoffman, daughter of a prosperous Baltimore merchant, received a telegram that utterly destroyed her life. She retreated to her bedroom immediately and for a year refused to come out. Her food and drink were placed on a tray outside her door. She permitted only one person to enter her room, her sister Dora. Day after day Dora read to Emily, almost ruining her eyes because Emily insisted that the room be kept in near darkness.

Dora read one letter in particular over and over to Emily. The letter had been sent to Emily by a man regarded by many as the very essence of coldness and cruelty; however, the letter was quite tender and touching, not cold nor cruel at all.

What news contained in the telegram caused Emily Hoffman to shut herself away for the world?

What prominent American wrote the tender letter to her?

ANSWERS

1. **THE OLDEST FORT:** The fort guards the city of St. Augustine, Florida. The people who raided St. Augustine in 1688 were from England. The Englishmen established the city of Charleston, South Carolina.

   Source: Randolph, Jack. "Forts of the Americas," *American Heritage,* March 1988, p. 84-86.

2. **WASHINGTON'S BIRTHDAY:** Actually Washington was born on February 11, 1732. Great Britain, including the American colonies, changed calendars in 1751, going from the Julian calendar to the Gregorian calendar. That caused a time difference of 11 days so that after 1751 Washington's birthday was February 22.

   Source: "Calendar," *Encyclopedia Brittanica*, sections on the Julian and Gregorian calendar.

3. **AN ENGLISH PREACHER:** The Englishman was named George Whitefield. He was a traveling preacher who was forced to speak in fields because ministers in America feared they would suffer in their congregations' comparison of Whitefield with them.

   The American who gave this money to Whitefield was Benjamin Franklin, and he writes of the incident in his *Autobiography.*

   The visit of Whitefield to America was termed "The Great Awakening." It brought a new and enthusiastic interest in religion.

   Source: Benjamin Franklin's *Autobiography.*

4. **THE FIRST TO DIE:** The man was named Crispus Attucks.

   The incident was the Boston Massacre.

   It occurred in 1770.

   This incident is considered by some historians as the beginning of the Revolutionary War although the war did not actually start until 1775.

   Source: The first paragraph quotation comes from "Chronicles of Negro Protest," compiled and edited by Bradford Chambers.

The second paragraph quotation comes from "Eyewitness: The Negro in American History," by William L. Katz.
Both paragraphs are quoted in *Annual Editions Readings in American History,* Vol. 2, Dushkin Publishing Group, Inc., Guilford, CT, 1973, p. 12.

5. **THE EMBLEM:** The rattlesnake is the creature written about.

Benjamin Franklin was the author.

The "Rattlesnake Flag" which bears a picture of an uncoiling snake with the words "Don't Tread on Me" under it was created.

Source: Franklin, Benjamin. "The Rattlesnake as a Symbol of America," *Pennsylvania Journal,* December 27, 1775.

6. **AMERICA'S POLISH REVOLUTIONARY:** According to a widely held legend, when he was a young man Kosciusko fell in love with a beautiful girl whose father violently disliked him. Kosciusko and the girl ran off to get married. Her father and his soldiers pursued the couple, caught them, recaptured the girl, wounded Kosciusko badly, and left him for dead. When Kosciusko regained consciousness, he found his lover gone and the only thing of hers remaining to him her handkerchief soaked in his blood.

Knowing that certain death awaited him if he remained in Poland, he fled, going first to Paris and later to America.

Is it possible that if a young Polish military engineer had not fallen in love with a beautiful girl whose father hated him, America might not have won the Revolutionary War, and we might still be part of the British empire?

Source: Froncek, Thomas. "Kosciusko," *American Heritage,* June 1975, p. 4-11, 78-81.

7. **A FOUNDING FATHER:** Alexander Hamilton.

In August 1772 a terrible hurricane struck the island of St. Croix in the Danish West Indies where Hamilton lived. Then 17 years old, Hamilton wrote a letter describing the storm to send to his father, but first he showed the letter to the Reverend Hugh Knox, a Presbyterian clergyman. The letter impressed Knox so much that he had it printed in a newspaper and decided that the boy was so intelligent that he must have a college education. Knox then raised the money necessary to send Hamilton off to New York City to attend King's College (now Columbia University).

Had there been no hurricane in St. Croix, the history of the United States might be quite different today.

Source: Miller, John C. *Alexander Hamilton: Portrait in Paradox,* Harper, NY, 1959.

8. **POPULATING A CONTINENT:** Before the American colonists won their independence from England the colonies had served as a dumping ground for English convicts. After the American victory Australia, a continent 14,000 miles from England's shores, became the new penal colony. The practice of sending convicts to a far land was called "transportation."

Source: Ward, Geoffrey C., "Hard Looks at American History," *American Heritage,* July/August 1987, p. 12-14.

9. **SLAVE AND ANTI-SLAVE:** The inventor was Eli Whitney.

He developed the cotton gin which made cotton a very valuable crop, and he sought to develop interchangeable parts which made mass production possible. Because the North had the means to mass produce weapons of war, it had a considerable advantage over the South where mass production was not as developed.

Source: Baida, Pater. "Eli Whitney's Other Talent," *American Heritage,* May/June 1987, p. 22-23.

10. **THE GREAT LEADER:** The great leader's name was Tecumseh.

He sought to put together a confederation of Indian nations to resist the white man's taking of their land.

He was able to predict an eclipse because he had enough knowledge of science to know when it would occur.

Tecumseh joined the British forces to fight the Americans during the War of 1812. He was killed near Lake Erie on October 5, 1813.

Source: Jarrett, Walter. "Tecumseh: The First Advocate of Red Power," *Mankind Magazine,* 1971.

11. **A TREASURED PRODUCT:** Ice. Before the invention of refrigerators or air conditioners, Tudor, Austin, and Rogers ran a company which cut large blocks of ice from New England lakes during the winter and shipped those blocks of ice packed in straw to prevent melting to India where that country's oppressively hot climate made ice a most treasured product.

Source: Sloane, Eric. "Natural Ice," *American Heritage*, August 1966, p. 83.

12. **CURED BY LOVE:** Sophia's maiden name was Sophia Peabody.

Her married name was Sophia Hawthorne.

Nathaniel Hawthorne was her husband.

Elizabeth and Mary Peabody were Sophia's sisters.

Mary was married to Horace Mann, the father of American education.

Source: Marshall, Megan. "Three Sisters Who Showed the Way," *American Heritage*, September/October 1987, p. 59-66.

13. **THE PECULIAR PEOPLE:** They were called Shakers. Begun in the United States in 1774 by an English woman named Ann Lee, the Shakers came to have 18 villages in eight states by 1826. They were called Shakers because of a strange dance that they performed as part of their religious ceremonies.

Source: Burns, Amy Stechler and Burns, Ken. *The Shakers: Hands to Work, Hearts to God,* Aperture, Inc., NY.

14. **FRIENDS OR ENEMIES:** The ex-President was Andrew Jackson.

The Missouri Senator was Thomas Hart Benton.

On September 4, 1813, after a falling out, Jackson and Benton abetted by several lieutenants engaged in a wild shootout during which Benton was slightly injured but during which Jackson was so severely wounded that he almost died. Of course, as you see, they later reconciled.

The very famous relative of the Missouri Senator was his namesake, Thomas Hart Benton, a leading American artist.

"The Battle of New Orleans" was the name of the song.

Source: Smith, Elbert B. "Now Defend Yourself, You Damned Rascal," *American Heritage*, February 1958, p. 44-47, 106.

15. **AMERICA'S GREATEST ORATOR:** We know this remarkable woman as Sojourner Truth. She had grown up a slave, and when her master, a man named Dumont, refused to honor the law that said she was to be freed on July 4, 1827, she fled from bondage. As a free woman, she filed the suits mentioned. It was utterly remarkable that a woman who had been a slave, a penniless Afro-American woman, should prevail against wealthy white men, but she did.

As Sojourner Truth, Isabella Van Wagener became one of the leading figures in the Abolitionist movement to free all slaves.

The book about her life was entitled *Narrative of Sojourner Truth.* After the Civil War broke out, she sought to obtain supplies for Afro-American troops, and to honor her work President Lincoln received her at the White House.

Source: Wallechinsky, David and Wallace, Irving. *Peoples' Almanac #2,* Wm Morrow and Co., Inc., NY, 1978.

16. **A GIFT FOR HIS PEOPLE:** His name was Sequoyah.

He had noticed that white men could communicate through the use of "signs" (that is, they could read and write).

He had spent the years creating and perfecting an alphabet for his people, one that gave them the means to communicate by reading and writing.

Source: Wallechinsky, David and Wallace, Irving. *Peoples' Almanac #1,* Doubleday and Co., Inc., Garden City, NY, 1975.

17. **THE INVENTION:** The artist was Samuel F. B. Morse.
He invented the telegraph.
Miss Ellsworth wrote, "What Hath God Wrought?"

Source: Prime, Samuel. *The Life of Samuel F. B. Morse,* The Ayer Publishing Co., Inc., Salem, NH, 1974.

18. **AMERICA'S PASTIME:** In rounders "outs" were made by *throwing* the ball at baserunners and hitting them; therefore, the ball had to be soft so it would not hurt the runner; thus, the ball could not be hit hard; it was not hard to catch; it could not

be thrown fast; in short, it did not challenge the players' physical abilities.

But if "outs" could be made by *tagging* the baserunners, then the ball could be hard. The speed and vigor of the game could be multiplied several times, and the ability of players to hit, throw, catch, and run could be fully tested.

And so baseball was born.

Source: Gordon, John Steele. "The American Game," *American Heritage,* April 1991, p. 19-20.

19. **IMMORTALITY IS A FIFTEEN MINUTE POEM:** Sarah Hale was the woman.

She wrote, "Mary had a Little Lamb."

Source: Hill, Ralph Nading. "Mrs. Godey's Lady," *American Heritage,* October 1958, p. 2-22, 97-101.

20. **THE RECLUSE AND THE LETTER:** Miss Emily Hoffman was engaged to General James McPherson, a Union commander. The telegraph notified her that he had been killed in action at the siege of Atlanta.

The letter had been written by General William T. Sherman, McPherson's superior officer, who had cared for McPherson as much as if the younger general had been his own son.

Source: Lord, Walter. "General Sherman and the Baltimore Belle," *American Heritage*, April 1958, p. 102-104.